Retrograde

Ryan Calais Cameron

methuen | drama
LONDON • NEW YORK • OXFORD • NEW DELHI • SYDNEY

METHUEN DRAMA
Bloomsbury Publishing Plc, 50 Bedford Square, London, WC1B 3DP, UK
Bloomsbury Publishing Inc, 1385 Broadway, New York, NY 10018, USA
Bloomsbury Publishing Ireland, 29 Earlsfort Terrace, Dublin 2,
D02 AY28, Ireland

BLOOMSBURY, METHUEN DRAMA and the Methuen
Drama logo are trademarks of Bloomsbury Publishing Plc.

First published in Great Britain 2023, this updated edition published in 2025

Copyright © Ryan Calais Cameron, 2023, 2025

Ryan Calais Cameron has asserted their right under the Copyright, Designs
and Patents Act, 1988, to be identified as Author of this work.

For legal purposes the Acknowledgements on p. vii
constitute an extension of this copyright page.

Cover design: Dewynters

Cover image © Hugo Glendinning

All rights reserved. No part of this publication may be: i) reproduced or
transmitted in any form, electronic or mechanical, including photocopying,
recording or by means of any information storage or retrieval system without
prior permission in writing from the publishers; or ii) used or reproduced in
any way for the training, development or operation of artificial intelligence (AI)
technologies, including generative AI technologies. The rights holders
expressly reserve this publication from the text and data mining exception as
per Article 4(3) of the Digital Single Market Directive (EU) 2019/790.

Bloomsbury Publishing Plc does not have any control over, or responsibility
for, any third-party websites referred to or in this book. All internet addresses
given in this book were correct at the time of going to press. The author and
publisher regret any inconvenience caused if addresses have changed or sites
have ceased to exist, but can accept no responsibility for any such changes.

No rights in incidental music or songs contained in the work are hereby
granted and performance rights for any performance/presentation
whatsoever must be obtained from the respective copyright owners.

All rights whatsoever in this play are strictly reserved and application
for performance etc. should be made before rehearsals begin to
Julia Tyrrell Management Ltd, 57 Greenham Road, London
N10 1LN, (info@jtmanagement.co.uk). No performance may
be given unless a licence has been obtained.

A catalogue record for this book is available from the British Library.

Library of Congress Control Number: 2025932234

ISBN: PB: 978-1-3505-6816-7
ePDF: 978-1-3505-6817-4
eBook: 978-1-3505-6818-1

Series: Modern Plays

Typeset by Mark Heslington Ltd, Scarborough, North Yorkshire
Printed and bound in Great Britain.

For product safety related questions contact
productsafety@bloomsbury.com.

To find out more about our authors and books visit
www.bloomsbury.com and sign up for our newsletters.

Retrograde originally opened at The Kiln Theatre on 20 April 2024, before transferring to the West End's Apollo Theatre on 8 March 2025 with the following cast and creative team:

CAST

Sidney	Ivanno Jeremiah
Parks	Stanley Townsend
Bobby	Oliver Johnstone
Understudy Bobby/Parks	James Alper
Understudy Sidney	Brett Curtis

CREATIVE TEAM

Writer	Ryan Calais Cameron
Director	Amit Sharma
Set & Costume Designer	Frankie Bradshaw
Lighting Designer	Amy Mae
Sound Designer	Beth Duke
Casting Director	Juliet Horsley
Associate Director	Rachael Nanyonjo
Associate Designer	Delyth Evans
Production Manager	Igor
Costume Supervisor	Isobel Pellow
Wigs, Hair and Make Up Supervisor	Suzanne Scotcher
Props Buyer	Charlotte King
Voice Coach	Hazel Holder

COMPANY

Company Stage Manager	Constance Oak
Company Stage Manager	Rike Bg
Deputy Stage Manager (Sound Operator)	Caroline Meer
Assistant Stage Manager (Book Cover)	Odette Robertson
Head of Wardrobe	Chris Cope

Head of Wigs	Pamela Ip
Producers	Colman Domingo and Nica Burns with Chuchu Nwagu Productions, New Frame Productions/Winnie Imara, Sayers & Sayers Productions, Tilted Productions, Holmes Steward Entertainment
General Manager	Laurence Miller
Assistant General Manager	Marissa Garbo
Production Coordinator	Alice Harvey
PR	Jo Allan PR
Marketing	Aaron McGregor Lucie Morgado Keshia Contini

The performance lasts approximately 90 minutes with no interval.

First performance of this production:
Saturday 8 March 2025.

For Nimax Theatres

Proprietors	NICA BURNS AND MAX WEITZENHOFFER
Chairman	MAX WEITZENHOFFER
Chief Executive	NICA BURNS
Company Secretary	MARC HUTCHINSON
Executive Director	JOAN MOYNIHAN
Commercial Director	LAURENCE MILLER
Finance Director	TONY YOE
Operations Director	GEOFF SUMMERTON
Head of Finance	FAY DIGGINS
Theatres Consultant	IAN ALBERY
General Counsel	ANDREW CLAYTON
General Manager, Production	SUSANNE NOBLE
Asst. General Manager, Production	
Concerts & Hires Manager	MARISSA GARBO
Head of Experience	JAMES CHARLTON
Head of Operations	GRACE CHRISTIE
Operations Coordinator	REBECCA DAY
Head of Buildings	NEIL LAGDEN
Buildings Manager	TONY LAMBERT
Buildings Administrator	DIANA PEREZ
Head of HR	NICOLA LITTLEWOOD
Business Administrator	LAUREN SHIELDS
Head of Ticketing	HATTI SIMPSON
Box Office Operations Manager	JASON OSBORNE
External Sales Manager	DANIEL SWAN
Ticketing Systems Manager	JOSÉ MORALES
Ticketing Systems Manager	CRAIG SULLIVAN-MOON
Audience Data & Insights Manager	EMMA TAYLOR
Groups & Education Sales Manager	SOPHIE DART
Access Manager	LAURA-JANE GARVIE
External Sales & Groups Officer	MATT STACEL
Groups & Access Sales Officer	MARK NOLAN
Ticketing & Box Office Administrator	ADAM DOLAN
Financial Accountant	WAYNE YOUNG
Management Accountant	LIZZIE NATHANIELSZ
Management Accountant	VANESSA KONG

Assistant Accountant	RENATA AVILA
Accounts Payable Officer	ELEANOR BROOKER
Payroll Coordinator	KIRSTY GIBSON
EA to Nica Burns	STEPHANIE CREED
EA to Nica Burns	GEMMA YIANNI
Marketing Manager	LUCIE MORGADO
Marketing Manager	AARON MCGREGOR
Design & Digital	MARC MURPHY
Social Media Officer	SOPHIE LING
Production Coordinator	ALICE HARVEY
Operations Administrator	JENNIFER HOARE
Reception	SARAH MORRIS
Reception	LUCIA RODRIGUEZ VAZQUEZ

For Apollo Theatre

Theatre Manager – *Michael Bond*
Assistant Theatre Manager – *Leigh Spence*
Duty Manager – *Ladeja Lammie*
Theatre Operations Supervisor – *Dani Jones*
Theatre Operations Supervisor – *Caitlyn McGuinness*
Theatre Operations Supervisor – *Emily Willis*
Head of Electrics – *Nick Smith*
Deputy Head of Electrics – *Jen Jackson*
Senior Electrics Technician – *Chris Mangalaparathy*
Head of Stage – *Jim Paterson*
Deputy Head of Stage – *Duncan Bailey*
Senior Stage Technician – *Amanda Vickers*
Box Office Supervisor – *Dan Carter*
Deputy Box Office Supervisor – *Nolan Meekings*
Box Office – *Zechariah O'Brien*
Stage Door – *Mourad Ghoumrassi*
Stage Door – *Kellie-Ann Richards*

Retrograde

Characters

Sidney, *Black, age 28, Transatlantic/well-spoken dialect. Intellectual demeanour. Calm, but can bite if provoked.*
Mr Parks, *age 50, New York accent. Confident, slick, manipulative. Larger than life.*
Bobby, *35, Liberal, needy, nerdy, go-getter.*

The stage has a misty feel to it, covered in the stench of rotten smoke, covering a 1950s-style office, with a liquor cabinet in tow.

A huge clock stands up on the opposite side of the room to the desk.

Jazz music playing in the background.

Bobby *and* **Mr Parks** *sit with cigarettes in hand and half-empty brandy glasses in show. It is clear that both men have had a few to drink and are very animated and jovial.*

Mr Parks Five in the morning?

Bobby Eastern time.

Mr Parks Sylvester Weaver, head of NBC?

Bobby (*sarcastically*) No the other one.

Mr Parks I just find it hard to believe the Head of NBC would have time to even look a schmuck like you in the eyes.

Bobby Looking me in the eyes is the least he could do, I've had my nose in his ass for the last ten years.

Mr Parks So he says?

Bobby 'Bobby Bobby'/

Mr Parks Right?/

Bobby 'I looked up that Sidney kid'/

Mr Parks Right?/

Bobby 'He's . . . he's . . .'

Mr Parks What? Spit it already.

Bobby He's a Black.

Mr Parks He must have had a fright!

Bobby He says, 'Bobby, son, he's not even Harry Belafonte Black. He's black-black!'

Mr Parks Oh shit, double black.

Bobby Double black!

The men laugh.

Mr Parks What did you say?

Bobby I said, well of course!

Mr Parks Bobby you're one crazy cat.

Bobby WOOF, WOOF, MEOW!!!

Mr Parks Brass balls, they should call ya', *Bobby brass balls*.

Bobby Thank you.

Mr Parks Where you grow those balls, son?

Bobby I had nothing to lose, right?

Mr Parks You've lost me.

Bobby You saw my episode of Mister Peepers?

Mr Parks Hey I'm just here to get shit signed and mind my damn business. Page 35 and 39 please.

Bobby You heard, everybody heard.

Mr Parks Minding my damn business, Bobby. 35 and/

Bobby Well it was shit.

Mr Parks So shit! Shit the bed type shit!

Bobby Hey!

Mr Parks You said it.

Bobby I can say it. You said you didn't see it.

Mr Parks Wish I hadn't.

Bobby Get Bent!

Mr Parks Anytime sweetie.

Bobby I had spent five years of my life kissing the same ass that was shitting on me, and I finally get to write my own episode, only to get a phone call and it's like, 'Everybody go home, it's going to be a fucking fire sale.'

Mr Parks *laughs out loud.* **Bobby** *is dead serious.*

Bobby Parks? After all these years, what do you think of me, be honest?

Mr Parks I never think of you Bobby, sorry.

Bobby What do you think they think of me, NBC, the industry, your kind of people?

Mr Parks 35 and 39, hurry up you're burning daylight.

Bobby When I think of my career to date/

Mr Parks I. don't. care/

Bobby I don't think of my feet on the chair in front of me with a strong whiskey in my hand having my feel of working with the best that the silver screen has to offer. I feel like a dime waiting for a dollar. I'm almost ten years deep in this and nobody is calling my name/

Mr Parks OK that's wonderful/

Bobby No respect, they should be mentioning me in the same breath as Budd Schulberg, or Paul Osborn.

Mr Parks UH-HUH.

Bobby It's all about to change. This one feels/

Mr Parks Good for you.

Bobby Gonna try something different/

Mr Parks That's right.

Bobby Radical people gonna talk about this for years/

Mr Parks Nice going, kid.

Bobby Are you listening?

Mr Parks Listen, me pretending to listen should be good enough.

Bobby People round here thought by now I would be sitting in the gutter feeding off a diet of rat tails and cockroach eggs, too depressed to care about the taste, but I'm back, baby. This script I've written is gonna blow away the doubters. It's provocative, but not provocative for the sake of being provocative type shit, but provocative, thank God it's provocative-provocative, you know what I'm trying to say? People are hungry for films like this, films that make them think. It's of the times, Parks, it's ahead of the times. I'm an auteur or a visionary.

Mr Parks *begins to clap.*

Bobby Thank you.

Mr Parks I'm not clapping cos I liked what you said I'm clapping cos you're finally done saying it!

Bobby *leafs through the pages and signs. Then starts to kiss the contract.*

Mr Parks What's he done?

Bobby Who?

Mr Parks The Black-Black.

Bobby *Blackboard Jungle* is his 'mini-break'.

Mr Parks The Richard Brooks' joint?

Bobby Bet ya bottom dollar.

Mr Parks Who'd he play?

Bobby You mean you ain't seen it, everybody's seen it!

Mr Parks If I'd seen it why ask?

Bobby One of the high school kids.

Mr Parks Good?

Bobby The breakout star!

Mr Parks Says who?

Bobby *The Times* says he was 'incredible, as effective when he had words to say as when he was silent'.

Mr Parks Shiiiit! You recite it like you wrote it.

Bobby If only I got there first.

Mr Parks So he's the real deal?

Bobby Most definitely. He's restrained, courteous, a classy guy, his heart is 18 carats. You'll see.

Mr Parks And you're tight?

Bobby Tighter than tight, I'll jump a bullet for that guy.

Mr Parks Psshh – If you got time to jump, he's got time to move.

Bobby We go way back, we used to gather our wives and tune in to NBC every Saturday night. I always said to Sid, if they ever give me a shot at another prime-time NBC gig, I'll put you in the picture. And now look, only a few days away from/

Mr Parks All of that for a Black-Black?

Bobby How'd you mean . . .?

Silence.

Mr Parks *laughs.*

Mr Parks You skinny little Beatniks always looking for new ways to defy the rules.

Bobby Look/

Mr Parks Troublemaker?

Bobby Huh?

Mr Parks If you can *Huh* you can hear.

Bobby No!

Mr Parks Sure?

Bobby I mean he can speak but/

Mr Parks Out of turn?

Bobby He's a good kid, Mr Parks.

Mr Parks Rumor has it he turned down the Phoenix project/

Bobby Who's Rumor and why she have it that way?

Mr Parks Hey comedian. Why didn't he do it?

Bobby I don't know.

Mr Parks You saying you don't know because you do know?

Bobby I'm saying I don't know because I don't know, if I did know I'll say I do know.

Mr Parks So you don't know.

Bobby No! But he doesn't like to talk about it.

Mr Parks You mean you give him a choice?

Bobby . . .

Mr Parks Where's he from?

Bobby Harlem.

Mr Parks Oh yea?

Bobby Well Florida, he moved from Florida, well the Bahamas, he moved to Florida from the Bahamas.

Mr Parks Does he hold American values, Bobby?

Bobby American/

Mr Parks You know what I'm talking about . . .

Silence.

Bobby *looks concerned and takes a sip of his drink.*

The two men eyeball one another.

The phone rings.

Mr Parks *picks it up and answers.*

Mr Parks (*into the phone*)   Hello . . . OK . . . Great, thank you.

Mr Parks *hangs up the phone.*

Mr Parks   Your guy is on the way up now.

Bobby   Great!

Mr Parks   Feel free to open the door and push yourself through it, and remember, if your phone doesn't ring, it's me.

Bobby *walks towards the door then stops in his tracks.*

Bobby   I might stick around for a minute or two.

Mr Parks   What's the situation?

Bobby   Just wanna settle him in, you know?

Mr Parks   Settle him in? Why not give him a sponge bath whilst you're at it?

Bobby   I'm a familiar face that's all.

Mr Parks   And what am I, chopped liver? . . .

Bobby   It's a big moment for the guy. I wanna stay and have a drink, a celebratory drink.

Mr Parks   Another one? You got champagne taste on a beer budget!

Bobby   Please, it would mean a lot to him . . .

Silence.

Mr Parks   OK. Settle him in. For a minute or two. Then kick rocks, I got work to do.

Bobby Thank you Mr Parks.

Mr Parks I don't even wanna know that you're here. I do the talking from here on in.

Bobby *puts his thumbs up, indicating 'yes'.*

Mr Parks *puts his cigarette in his mouth whilst doing a little dance.*

Checks his tie and his suit in the mirror.

Bobby *pours another drink.*

There are two loud knocks on the door.

Mr Parks *takes a look at the clock, then slicks his hair back and sits back in the chair with cigarette in tow like he owns the whole building.*

Mr Parks Who's there/

Bobby Come in!!

Mr Parks What did I just say/

Sidney *enters.*

Sidney Good morning/

Bobby/Mr Parks Good morning!

Sidney . . . I'm here to see a man about a dog.

Bobby Well I'm *the man*, so that must make him the/

Sidney *and* **Bobby** *burst out in a fit of laughter.*

Sidney Bobby, I didn't know you would still be here.

Mr Parks That makes two of us.

Bobby Heard you were in next and thought, maybe we could take the subway back uptown together?

Sidney That's fine by me, oh and whilst I have you here, I've been going over the script again and Bobby I must say, I've never come across/

Mr Parks *coughs intentionally.*

Mr Parks What's buzzin, cuzzin? What's the story morning glory? What's your tale nightingale?

Sidney and **Bobby** *look at one another then burst out laughing.*

Bobby How rude of me, Mr Parks this is my friend Sidney Poitier who speaks regular English, and Sidney this is studio executive lawyer, Mr Larry Parks.

Mr Parks Mr Parks will do.

Bobby They say there are three things certain in life – death, taxes and Mr Parks getting contracts signed.

Mr Parks Poitier, just tell him not to use the word genius whilst describing me, I blush easily.

Sidney Noted. A pleasure to meet you Mr Parks.

Mr Parks Not at all, the pleasure is mine.

Sidney That's very kind.

Mr Parks Your reputation precedes you.

Sidney Bobby what have you said, how much do I owe you?

Bobby Too much, Sidney, too much.

They laugh.

Mr Parks I'm a huge fan of yours. I loved Black boys' jingle/

Bobby *Board Jungle/*

Mr Parks I particularly like the review that said you were as effective when you had words to say as when you were silent/

Bobby Hey!

Sidney Well. Let's just see how this next project goes hey?

Mr Parks You don't like a compliment, kid?

Sidney Err . . . no . . . I suppose I just don't want to like it too much.

Bobby I like that, don't you like that Parks?

Sidney I thought after *Blackboard Jungle* things would be really picking up but I've spent most of the time out of work or/

Bobby Playing thugs or servants/

Sidney Who have no names or no lives. Three or four scenes, you're not going to be able to show what you can do. A little bitty pay-check, and then you're going to be hungry for your next role which is absolutely the same.

Bobby Sid's had to run a ribs restaurant on the side.

Sidney More like a little hole in the wall, eighty cents a meal, including side dishes/

Mr Parks You had me at eighty cents a meal son.

Bobby Best ribs in Harlem!

Sidney Just something to support the family between movie assignments, you know. Honestly, this is a dream job that's come at the best possible time for us.

Bobby Sid's got two little grasshoppers and another on the way! A proper hard-working, law-abiding-immigrant, family man, right Sid? You're the American dream pal. Tell the man.

Mr Parks Congratulations and commiserations on the incoming hellraiser. Take a seat, loosen your jaw, and rattle your bones for a while hey? G'head get comfortable will ya.

Sidney Thank you sir.

Mr Parks Drinks! Where. Are. My. Manners? (*To* **Bobby**.) go get us some clean glasses.

Bobby Excuse me.

Mr Parks You're excused.

Bobby What am I, Cinderella? I don't work for you.

Mr Parks Do you want to work ever again?

The two men eyeball one another.

Bobby *gets up from his seat and makes his way to the liquor cabinet.*

Mr Parks And grab the special label Dalmore whisky! (*To* **Sidney**.) This was a present from Alfred Hitchcock. In Britain, they call it Scotch, can you believe that, Scotch?

Sidney We're going to drink before the meeting? Don't you usually do that after?

Mr Parks Well how about we do both?

Sidney You know the alcohol is dehydrating so the more you drink the hotter you're going to feel.

Mr Parks Wow.

Sidney Yes.

Mr Parks How are you doing that?

Sidney/Bobby What?

Mr Parks Such a good impression of my old lady!

Bobby *laughs.*

Mr Parks (*mimicking*) Liquor is very bad Larry!

Sidney *checks his watch.*

Mr Parks You in a rush?

Sidney No, well, yes . . . kind of . . . I have to open up shop, and then my wife is cooking lunch it's/

Mr Parks Sounds like a keeper, Poitier! We all know it takes face powder to catch a man but baking powder to keep him!

Mr Parks *and* **Bobby** *laugh.* **Sidney** *has a face of thunder.*

Sidney   Well I said I wouldn't be long; I'm just coming in to sign my contracts/

Mr Parks   You wanna call your wife right now and ask her if she's mixed up your trousers in the laundry? You're worrying the balls off a brass monkey.

Bobby   Mi casa es su casa, Sidney.

Mr Parks   Exactly. What do we work so hard for, Poitier? To buy our wives the best rolling pins so we can live life out here right. Am I right or am I right?

Bobby   Too right! Three right!

Mr Parks   Best things in life make you either fat, drunk, or pregnant.

Bobby   My wife was all three at one point!

Mr Parks   Take off that goddamn suit jacket and relax, I feel like I'm shitting on Mercury just looking at you.

Bobby *arrives with the bottle of whiskey, three glasses and an ice bucket.*

Mr Parks *pours into the three glasses.*

Sidney   I hope you won't be offended if I have one on the city?

Bobby   How'd you mean?

Mr Parks   Water, he thinks he can drink water in this office.

Sidney   I'm hot, it's a hot day.

Bobby   Sidney?

Sidney   What Bobby?/

Mr Parks   I can't trust a man that doesn't drink/

Bobby Don't be silly; Mr Parks has enough liquor to kill a horse.

Mr Parks What's the matter, you Amish?

Sidney It's too early.

Mr Parks My office doesn't have opening hours. We're all functioning drunks here.

Bobby Come on Sid, it's 5 o'clock somewhere in the world.

Sidney I just desire doing business with a sober mind/

Mr Parks No one desires doing business with a sober mind. Do you know how tedious this shit is?

Bobby Look I suppose Sidney can just/

Mr Parks You always act that way?/

Sidney What way?/

Mr Parks He always act that way?/

Bobby I don't know, ask him, he's in front of ya/

Sidney What way?/

Mr Parks Like an old fuddy-duddy rolling around in your Daddy's button-up suit, talking like, like The Queen of England's husband.

Sidney The King of England?

Mr Parks Him too. Lemme tell you something, kid, you need to create a persona out here.

Sidney What's wrong with the one I have?

Mr Parks Stale.

Sidney What? Bobby?

Bobby Hmm.

Sidney Stale?

Bobby I don't know, maybe, maybe/

Mr Parks The truth Bobby! If he's your pal tell him the truth!

Bobby OK, OK. Look, yea maybe you can loosen up a little you know?

Mr Parks You're being a drip, Poitier.

Bobby No need for that/

Mr Parks You're a drip and you're drip, drip, dripping all over my floor.

Sidney Sorry I/

Mr Parks You're flooding my damn floor sweetheart.

Sidney OK sir!

Mr Parks Maria!!! Maria!!!

Bobby Maria?

Sidney There's no Maria.

Mr Parks We need a clean-up on office 102.

Sidney Your point has been made/

Mr Parks I got Sidney Poitier in here acting like he was raised in a nunnery for grandpas!!!

Bobby *attempts to hold back his own laughter.*

Sidney I'll have a drink! Please? Thank you, Mr Parks.

Mr Parks Ayyyyyyyeee you're cooking with gas now Poitier.

Bobby Nice one Sidney, good look pal.

Mr Parks (*jesting*) I never gave up hope, Poitier.

Sidney *laughs.*

Mr Parks (*to* **Sidney**) Fun looks good on you, kid. Smile whilst you still have teeth.

Sidney A toast?

Bobby/Mr Parks A toast!

Mr Parks More gain for all us real pals, and more pain for all our sham pals!

Bobby Salute!

Mr Parks/Sidney Salute!!!

The men clap glasses together and begin to drink.

Sidney *almost chokes on his drink.*

Mr Parks Good?

Sidney Wow, yes good.

Mr Parks Good!

Sidney Yea good.

Bobby/Mr Parks Good!!

Sidney Goooood!

Bobby Gooood.

Sidney Goooood!

Bobby/Sidney Gooooood!

Mr Parks OK, calm down, I said functioning drunks, emphasis on the functioning.

They all laugh.

Sidney Sincerest apologies, I skipped breakfast.

Sidney *lets out a huge burp then continues to drink before* **Mr Parks** *gives him a refill.*

Mr Parks Listen, some advice. You youngsters need to consider 'what am I going to give,' not 'what am I going to get.' Most people come to this industry cos' they want something. This industry will not respond to you unless you are ready to give, to make a sacrifice . . . Now gimme that damn tie son. Loosen up, we here celebrating, loosen up.

Sidney *laughs then takes off his tie.*

Bobby *and* **Mr Parks** *give* **Sidney** *a round of applause.*

Sidney *steadies himself, takes a seat, then checks his watch.*

Sidney   My agent said that the contracts have been/

Mr Parks   Marty Baum?

Sidney   Yes.

Mr Parks   I love that guy, booked you the Phoenix project, right?

Bobby   Mr Parks?

Sidney   Marty suggested me/

Mr Parks   What a great job!/

Bobby   Mr Parks.

Mr Parks   I must say you turned out a performance and a half as per usual.

Bobby   Mr Parks??

Sidney   I wasn't in the movie.

Mr Parks   You weren't?

Sidney   No sir.

Bobby   Mr Parks.

Mr Parks   I'm so sorry I've confused you.

Sidney   Must have been the other Negro actor.

Mr Parks   It's just that you said Marty suggested you, you booked it? But you didn't make the film? How peculiar, no?

Sidney Excuse me?

Bobby Mr Parks!

Mr Parks Say my name one more time, kid!!!

Bobby . . . Sidney doesn't like to talk about it.

Mr Parks Sidney doesn't have a mouth?

Sidney Sidney doesn't like to talk about it.

Mr Parks I'm sorry, don't talk about if you don't want, but if you feel like you want to then please go ahead.

Sidney Thank you.

Mr Parks So?

Sidney So?

Bobby So what?

Mr Parks Tell me!

Sidney How did you hear about it?

Mr Parks Industry isn't as big as you think, kid. Everybody knows somebody that knows somebody that knows everybody, and some people talk, and some people listen.

Bobby And some people pretend they didn't hear, but they did.

Mr Parks And some people want a knuckle sandwich express delivery. Come on, Poitier . . . we're all buddies here, now aren't we?

Sidney *considers.*

Mr Parks *stares intently.*

Sidney The role was a janitor, to which I had no objection. This janitor worked for a gambling casino. Someone connected with his company was killed, and it was thought that the janitor had information about the death. The people who perpetrated the crime went to the janitor and said, 'It is imperative that you don't speak of whatever you may know.' Then they killed his daughter. They threw her body on his lawn, and he didn't do anything.

Mr Parks/Bobby OK . . .?

Sidney OK???

Mr Parks So why turn it down, what's wrong with it?

Sidney He was enraged. He was tormented. Still, he remained passive. He didn't do anything for himself. He just left it to other people to fight his battles for him. I could not imagine playing that part. I told my agent that I couldn't play the role. He never understood.

Mr Parks And you're telling me, big ugly me, that you turned it down cos your make-believe daughter gets whacked?

Sidney Yes, I mean no, I mean/

Mr Parks Who advised you?

Bobby Advised him?

Sidney On what?

Mr Parks On what to do, what action to take?

Sidney I suppose the wisdom of my father and the courage of my mother and/

Mr Parks Pretty. Poetic, Bobby, you didn't tell me he was The Black Ginsberg.

Bobby Stop it.

Mr Parks I wanna know who sanctioned, supported, and subsidized you?

Sidney I don't understand.

Mr Parks What you think I'm nuts? You live in the ghetto and/

Sidney I do not live in the ghetto/

Mr Parks You expect me to believe you didn't have someone slipping dollars and cents into your back pocket, come on, who was it, Poitier?

The phone rings and after a few rings **Mr Parks** *picks it up.*

Mr Parks Hello? (*To the others.*) Excuse me.

Mr Parks *pulls the phone cord as far as he can to take this call.*

Sidney Bobby, what's going on here?

Bobby I guess he just wants you to feel welcome, you know? To feel like part of something big here, part of the NBC family.

Sidney Something doesn't feel right . . . Is it something I said?

Bobby I just don't feel like you have to say so much.

Sidney Please elaborate?

Bobby You don't want people thinking you're troublesome, or problematic.

Sidney I've hardly even/

Bobby It can be intimidating for a lot of these guys, they're not used to it, so up close and personal.

Sidney 'It'?

Bobby Hey, now come on, Sid.

Sidney Does your script not advocate change and/

Bobby Yes but/

Sidney Not too much change then?

Bobby Hey Sidney! Don't bust my balls on this, OK? You know, I'm conscious, I get it, I'm the blackest white guy you know.

Sidney (*in jest*) Don't ever say that again.

Bobby (*laughs*) We just gotta play the game a little. How about you show some Fun-Sidney?

Sidney Excuse me?

Bobby Bump gums with the guy.

Sidney I'm trying.

Bobby Maybe a story, an anecdote, something light? Just let the man know you're 'relatable', part of the culture here, you dig?

Sidney . . .

Bobby We're almost there, Sid . . . Remember I said we'll make a movie and we'll get that extra light on you, so it won't glare up on your skin. We gonna see you, Sid, all of you on prime-time television.

They both laugh.

Mr Parks *comes off the phone and looks up at the clock, then takes a breath. Then back into the conversation.*

Mr Parks OK, Bobby, time's up.

Bobby Sid was just telling me a story.

Mr Parks He was?

Sidney I was?

Bobby He was! About how one day you're a dishwasher and the next you're sitting in the offices of NBC about to play a lead role in a script written by one of the finest writers of his generation. G'head Sid, tell the man!

Sidney Yes . . . ha . . . So much of life seems to be determined by pure randomness. I had no money when I arrived in New York and I had no relatives, no friends. I was fifteen and I had to earn a living. My education was poor; I quit school at twelve-and-a-half.

Bobby How about we skip to the *fun part*, Sid!

Sidney Right! So, I'm looking in the Amsterdam newspaper for a dishwashing job. And there were none, but something on the opposite page caught my eye. Two words, 'Actors Wanted.' Very much like on the other page it said, 'Dishwashers Wanted' or 'Foreigners Wanted'.

Bobby *and* **Mr Parks** *laugh,* **Sidney** *is buoyed by the reaction and starts going for it.*

Sidney So I thought, 'Well I've been trying this dishwashing thing, I might as well see what this other thing is about.'

Bobby So what did you do?

Sidney I went!

The men laugh.

Sidney I knocked on the stage door and a guy opened – a big stout man, I said, 'Is this the place where the actors are wanted?' And he said, 'are you an actor?'

I said 'Of course,' (*He laughs.*)

He said, 'here's a script, turn to page 28'. This of course was the first problem I had because I had never heard the word 'script' before. He says, 'Why don't you go up on the stage and read the part of John?' I opened the book and there were a lot of names, 'John . . .' and underneath 'John' were words. Then there was another name and underneath that name were words. Well, I got it very quickly, I said, 'I better read what's under John.'

The men laugh.

Sidney Now I have to forewarn you that I was fresh from the Caribbean – but I mean fresh – and I had the worst Caribbean accent –

Bobby Or the best depending on how you look at it.

The men laugh.

Mr Parks Let's hear it!

Sidney Excuse me?

Bobby You have to, just a little piece, say bacon!

Sidney No way, I couldn't.

Mr Parks/Bobby Come on!/Go on Sidney/just a bit/come on!!!

Sidney (*Caribbean accent*) My name is Sidney Poitier and I'm from Cat Island in the Bahamas.

Bobby *and* **Mr Parks** *burst out laughing.*

Mr Parks What was that? How did he do that, that shit was incredible?

Bobby Encore, ENCORE.

Mr Parks He said 'Bahamas' . . . 'Bahama.'

Sidney Simple words would trip me up, so I was not going to rush or stumble. I said, 'And. So. John. Is. My. Name. Oh, yes,'

They all erupt into laughter.

Mr Parks What did the fat guy say?

Sidney Well I didn't get through the first speech. I heard 'slam!' That was his script slamming shut. He took me by my ear and started to lead me out. 'You can't be an actor with an accent like that, get out of here, go find a job as a dishwasher.'

Mr Parks (*laughs*) That's a sad story/

Bobby It's a tragedy/

Sidney I got to thinking, I didn't tell him that I was a dishwasher. Where would he get the notion to say that?

The men laugh louder.

Sidney So, I decided that I couldn't allow that to stand. I decided that I was going to be an actor.

Mr Parks In that moment?

Sidney In that damn moment!

The men laugh.

Sidney And I was going to prove to *him* that he was wrong about me. Then I'll walk away and give up this acting business because I don't want to be a stinking actor anyway.

The men laugh.

Mr Parks Poitier, you sure know how to tickle an old fella really good.

Bobby He's a hoot, right Parks?

Mr Parks You go back?

Sidney Damn straight! But I still had no money so I said, I would do the janitor works free for a whole year if they let me understudy . . . The lead role went to a young Harry Belafonte/

Mr Parks Belafonte?

Sidney You know him?/

Mr Parks Day-o, day-o!

Sidney/Bobby Daylight come, and we want go home.

Mr Parks Day, is a day, is a day, is a day, is a day, is a day-o.

Sidney/Bobby/Mr Parks Daylight come, and we want go home.

Sidney Voice of an angel.

Bobby Face of a demon!

Mr Parks Eat shit, Bobby.

Sidney Opening night they waited for Harry to get there, he was late, director said, 'Okay Sidney, would you get up and read the part until Harry arrives'.

Mr Parks Shit.

Bobby Shit.

Sidney Shit.

Mr Parks Well!?

Sidney I got up there and I played Harry's part!!! Harry didn't show all that evening!!!

Mr Parks Good show?

Sidney Terrible! I got scared, stumbled through, getting the lines all back to front and finally at the end of it I walked off, I walked home. At about 12 o'clock the press was released, ten of the thirteen newspapers trashed the show. But they asked, 'Who was that kid who came out there and just broke up the whole audience? He has perfect comedic timing,' I said, 'Wait a minute, wait a minute. That's me!!!'

They men laugh.

Sidney A Broadway director came and said to me, 'Come to my office on Monday. I'm going to do a production of *Lysistrata* and I'd like you to read.'

Mr Parks Bullshit.

Sidney Real shit!

Mr Parks You go?

Sidney I didn't sleep until Monday.

Mr Parks Well ring-a-ding-ding slap a giraffe! You get it?

Sidney Got it!

Mr Parks Good!

Mr Parks *bursts out laughing and gives* **Sidney** *a round of applause.*

Mr Parks Poitier, that was a blast!

Bobby Parks, I told you he was top dollar!

Sidney This is what I mean by 'so much of life is determined by pure randomness'. I happened to have been standing at the right place at the right time. If there had been another chap at that spot with a requisite set of qualifications, it would have been him.

Mr Parks You're a generational talent, Poitier, that is not random at all, that's a gift, you hear me? And I know you're a man of principle, but you're also a man, so I know you like the idea of nicer things.

Sidney What do you mean?

Mr Parks A pocket so full of dead presidents they'll call you Mount Rushmore. Racing down a country road in a Ford convertible with the roof down. Cold champagne and hot baths. Enjoying the company of attractive young women in low-cut gowns, looking like they're ready for open heart surgery, in the limited way a married man can. Whilst they glide into your lap like tropical fish in an aquarium. How's that sound to you?

Sidney *laughs.*

Sidney I don't know.

Bobby *(laughs)* You damn well know, Sidney!

They laugh.

Mr Parks Don't be impressed. This is nothing. The lead in one prime-time TV movie isn't impressive, Poitier, you know what is?

Sidney What?

Mr Parks A studio contract, you'll never have to work a day in your life again.

Sidney Yea well . . ./

Mr Parks That's where you're heading, kid. You're tall in New York, but you can be huge in Hollywood. MGM are headhunting you, to be their first Negro star, don't tell nobody you heard it from this body but it's the truth. I'm telling ya, money buys happiness and whoever disagrees never had enough of either.

Bobby *laughs whilst* **Sidney** *considers the fantasy, awestruck.*

Bobby You wouldn't even need the ribs restaurant anymore or even/

Mr Parks Small projects like this, no offence, Bobby. The whole world would be your oyster, but first they gotta know they can trust you, that you play by the rules, you see. Now that's what this is/

Mr Parks *goes to open his desk drawer.*

Bobby What do you mean by that?

Mr Parks What-what now?

Bobby 'Projects like this'.

Mr Parks I said no offence. Jheeze! If you're offended by the things I say, imagine the things I hold back.

Bobby Like what?

Sidney Bobby, let's just get signed up and go/

Mr Parks I don't wish to cause any . . . Outrage/

Bobby Outrage? What are people saying about this script, Parks?

Mr Parks Look I'm just here to do contracts, I ain't no chatty patty.

Bobby You've done nothing but chat all God damn morning.

Mr Parks Hey you little shit!

Sidney Bobby, let's concentrate on/

Bobby Hit me with it, Parks!

Mr Parks Calm your chassis, Bobby, I mean it.

Bobby I said hit me!

Mr Parks The character you play, Poitier/

Sidney Tommy/

Mr Parks He's just been ring-a-ding-dinging on my cranium you see.

Bobby Please enlighten me.

Mr Parks I couldn't help but feel like he was somewhat . . . (claps lips) unbelievable.

Bobby You shitting me?!

Sidney Bobby calm down.

Mr Parks Unrelatable you see. Like, Poitier, how would your people/

Sidney My people?/

Bobby His people?

Mr Parks Respond to a character that's so/

Sidney So?

Bobby So what?

Mr Parks (*smiles*) I don't know if we should go there, being right too soon is socially unacceptable nowadays.

Sidney We're already here.

Mr Parks The script has an unusual portrayal of an interracial friendship. It's weird, to be honest, kind of forced, you dig?

Sidney No I do not dig.

Mr Parks You going to stand there and tell me you're not astonished by Tommy/your character's authority on the harbour?

Sidney OK, now we're getting somewhere.

Mr Parks Come on, give me a bone here. Coloureds in positions of authority? What'd you make of that?

Sidney I quite like it.

Mr Parks Well of course you like it but/

Sidney Is it believable?/

Mr Parks You head a crew of white dockworkers who call you 'sir'. It's lacking in authenticity, and you ought to be careful of work like that as a young artist. I want more than this for you; you're better than silly liberal trite!

Bobby Liberal trite!

Mr Parks Hey I guess it does what it needs to do if you like that soppy shit, and NBC seem to like it . . . I just think your role as an artist should be to reflect the truth, no?

Sidney Who's truth, yours or mine?

Bobby Sidney, hold back/

Mr Parks Look, I know what you think and you're wrong to think that way. If I were any more open-minded my brain would fall out. I get the Negro problem but/

Sidney I don't think it's the Negro that has the problem/

Bobby Sidney!/

Mr Parks Hattie McDaniel in *Gone with the Wind*?

Sidney Hattie McDaniel . . .

Mr Parks Now I got callouses on my hands from how hard I clapped during her Oscar speech, 'It's better to play a maid then be a maid' – words straight from the horse's chops. You show me a house in the South that doesn't have a Negro maid and I'll show you a lie. She's a great actor, great writing, great character, everything was so/

Sidney Palatable?

Mr Parks Well no, I. Listen.

Sidney You didn't feel intimidated.

Bobby Sidney/

Mr Parks Look/

Sidney You wasn't confused.

Mr Parks OK, Poitier, bravo, let's just get back to/

Sidney I live in a country where I can't live where I want to live. I live in a country where I can't go where I want to eat. I live in a country where I can't get a job, except for those put aside for people of my colour or caste. I get an opportunity to be taken away from all of that and you prefer that I reenactor it? It appears that people like Mr Parks who are familiar with how things once were are petrified of how things could be.

Bobby Sidney!

Sidney It's fine, I've come to learn that certain Industry folk are very deliberate in creating a particular vision, then protecting and defending it.

Bobby Mr Parks, may we have that contract now please/

Mr Parks Let him cook!

Sidney When I got Bobby's script for *Ten Feet Tall*, I was on my phone to Marty. I was quickly leafing through the script. I'm like, 'Marty, I don't understand what the part is?' He says

'Buddy, it's Tommy, he's offered you Tommy.' I think about that moment a lot. I didn't even assume when being offered something, even from a friend, that I would be one of the central storytellers without caricature or stereotype. I love this script because it brings something otherworldly that people like yourself cannot even fathom. Mr Parks, this isn't just a movie it's a whole movement. Whether you like it or not is irrelevant. Get ready. We are coming. Expect us.

Mr Parks *chokes on his drink.*

Mr Parks There he is. SIDNEY POITIER . . . Welcome . . .

Silence.

Bobby Well, ha! This crazy damn heat, hey? Got everybody hot, and crazy!!!

Bobby *looks over at* **Sidney**, **Sidney** *looks back sheepishly.*

Bobby It's just a misunderstanding tell the man, Sidney.

Sidney . . . I . . .

Mr Parks Well it looks like your one or two minutes are up, Bobby. Mr Poitier looks very settled. Very settled indeed.

Bobby I . . . I think Sid would like if/

Mr Parks I think Poitier doesn't need no talking for. We all know how well he can talk.

Silence.

Bobby Sidney?

Sidney *nods his head 'OK' but looks uncomfortable, he knows he has overstepped the mark.*

Bobby OK, well I'll see you Monday, right? Ready for your camera tests . . . all signed up, right? This is our dream, Sid, and dreams don't work unless we do . . .

Silence.

Bobby *leaves.*

Sidney *is desperately looking for a way to atone for his outburst.*

Sidney   . . . As I'm sure you know, Mr Parks, it's very hard to be your own man in America, and sometimes we can get carried away with our own passions and inhibitions. Back home in the Bahamas everyone was Black, ha! I never had an occasion to question colour; I only saw myself as what I was . . . you know . . . a man. My mother and my father's son . . . Do you understand what I mean Mr Parks? I did not mean to offend you I just . . . I just really want to do this movie, it represents/

Mr Parks   You OK?

Sidney (*smiles*)   Yes . . . Sorry sir, I just wanted to/

Mr Parks   Amnesia sufferer?

Sidney   Excuse me?

Mr Parks   You forget. You forgot who you were, where you are, who I am, where I'm from, where you're from?/

Sidney   Sorry?/

Mr Parks   Don't forget that. Never forget that shit. That shit could save your life. These walls have ears and eyes and teeth. Teeth that would love to bite your Black ass given a chance. Don't forget that. You cannot afford amnesia. That's some expensive shit. So, don't get emotional, you are hired, fired, you hit a few marks, say a few lines, shut your mouth, get paid, get laid, simple shit, Poitier. The important thing to remember is not to forget. Got it?

Sidney   Got it.

Mr Parks   Good.

Sidney *sinks in his seat feeling lucky to still be here.*

Mr Parks *goes over to his desk drawer to retrieve two enveloped documents and turns off the music.*

Sidney   Yes, let's take a look at these contracts then, hey?

Mr Parks *makes his way back over to the table.*

Mr Parks They love your work out here, they're just not too keen on you.

Sidney What does that mean?

Mr Parks What did you think this meeting was about?

Sidney I thought I was here to sign an employment contract.

Mr Parks No terms of employment 'till we know whose side you're on.

Sidney 'Side?'

Mr Parks There's a whole war outside, Poitier, and we'll be damned if we let it propagate our television screens.

Sidney What are you talking about??

Mr Parks *slides over two enveloped documents for* **Sidney**.

Sidney *opens the first and begins to read it.*

Mr Parks A loyalty oath.

Sidney An oath.

Mr Parks That's right.

Sidney To what?

Mr Parks Not to what.

Sidney Then to whom?

Mr Parks OK Rogers and Hammerstein, let's not make a musical about it. Studios are adding clauses forbidding actors from committing any offence that will risk public hatred, contempt or ridicule. The industry is moving, it's evolving, but it's still fragile. The Big Daddies believe just a whiff of indecency or controversy can destroy the entire show.

Sidney OK, but what has this got to do with me/

Mr Parks They want to know, that if you should fall, you would bleed blue and not/

Sidney Red? . . . Really?

Mr Parks Senator McCarthy is getting tough on/

Sidney I'm just an actor!/

Mr Parks Activists!

Silence.

Mr Parks *takes out the contract and a document with sensitive information about* **Sidney**.

Mr Parks Truth is, you've been associated with people that have questionable characters.

Sidney What people?

Mr Parks Politically unacceptable persons.

Sidney And what accounts for/

Mr Parks People that are known for not holding American values/

Sidney . . .?

Mr Parks Troublemakers!

Sidney You want to tell me what's going on?

Mr Parks You want to tell me your affiliation with Harry Belafonte?

Sidney Harry?

Mr Parks You heard.

Sidney And you know, I told you/

Mr Parks What is your *affiliation* with Harry Belafonte?

Sidney This is embarrassing/

Mr Parks As embarrassing as you being blacklisted?

Sidney I need a lawyer.

Mr Parks I am your lawyer.

Sidney This goes against my 1st amendment right, are you aware of this?/

Mr Parks No studio will ever employ a member of the Communist Party, are you aware of this?

Sidney Harry's a buddy, OK; he's a pal of mine.

Mr Parks You were seen attending a private meeting with Mr Belafonte at the American Negro Theatre on February 12 is that right/

Sidney How would I/

Mr Parks Is. That. Right. Poitier?

Sidney YES SIR.

Mr Parks Would you care to reveal the details of said meeting.

Sidney No sir.

Mr Parks What were the details of said meeting?

Sidney We're old friends meeting with old friends talking about old shit I guess.

Mr Parks Can you confirm that you spoke about Martin Luther King Jr and raising money for the Montgomery bus boycott?

Sidney I do not have a trained memory.

Mr Parks Canada Lee. What was your affiliation with him?

Sidney He was a friend.

Mr Parks You took a job with him in 1952.

Sidney Yes, I've taken jobs with him.

Mr Parks Why did you choose to do that?

Sidney   Because I wanted to.

Mr Parks   Do you share the same political views as Canada Lee?

Sidney   What kind of/

Mr Parks   DO YOU SHARE/

Sidney   My views are my views and his were his. Now let the man's name rest in/

Mr Parks   Yet you were friends.

Sidney   Yes, that is possible.

Mr Parks   Would you agree that Mr Lee was strongly opposed to Senator McCarthy?

Sidney   McCarthy?/

Mr Parks   Would you agree?

Sidney   YES! Now where or whom are you getting this information from? This is/

Mr Parks   Can you confirm performing at the Paul Robeson benefit for the Jewish Anti-Fascist Committee?

Sidney   I went to support a friend, I didn't perform.

Mr Parks   Would you consider Robeson as a friend?

Sidney   Well yes/

Mr Parks   Do you agree with said statement from your friend: *'We in America do not forget that it was on the backs of the White workers from Europe and on the backs of millions of Blacks that the wealth of America was built. And we are resolved to share it equally. We shall not make war on anyone. We shall not make war on the Soviet Union!!!'*

Silence.

Sidney   . . . Look, it's taken/

Mr Parks   Do you agree?/

Sidney Out of context and ironic/

Mr Parks Do you/

Sidney For a country that prides itself in the concepts of personal liberty and freedom of political organization.

Mr Parks Poitier, are you a Communist?

Sidney This is an infringement on my constitutional rights and a violation of my freedom of speech.

Mr Parks Those rights have now been revoked from accused Communists as your actions present a clear and obvious danger to the American way of life.

Sidney I'm not a Communist, OK!

Mr Parks Prove it.

Sidney What??

Mr Parks Do you agree with Paul Robeson's comments?

Sidney No! Yes . . . I . . . I mean . . . No . . .

Mr Parks You speak of your values but seem to care very little about America's.

Sidney I . . . I . . . I . . . I.

Mr Parks You seem to have little concern for the damage that you/

Sidney Me?/

Mr Parks And your Communist friends are having, polluting the minds of our young through your films and television/

Sidney I'm not in any political party OK!

Mr Parks You are coming across as a man of many contradictions, Mr Poitier, we need to excavate the truth.

Sidney When I'm told that people's human rights are being threatened, and then asked to participate in a benefit or a rally, I'm always willing to lend my voice to the cause . . . It's only human, right?

Mr Parks Good. That's good enough for me, kid. Now we just need that in documentation form. For them.

Silence. **Mr Parks** *slides the Oath over to* **Sidney**.

Mr Parks This loyalty oath is the best I can do for you, it's protection. Lesson of the day is, lie down with dogs, get up with fleas. And right now, everyone thinks you're contagious.

Sidney Just where did you get that information from?

Mr Parks Just sign the/

Sidney Am I being watched?

Mr Parks Don't be ridiculous.

Sidney Am I being bugged? All this time I thought I was finding it hard to find work because I was Black, now I learn it was because someone told you I was red? Who was it? You got a spy?

Sidney *becomes so paranoid he gets up from his seat.*

Mr Parks Sit down!

Sidney An informant? You must have an informant?

Mr Parks Poitier, what did I say about knowing your place?

Sidney It only makes sense that it's someone I allowed into my home, close enough to break bread with me, they may have played in the yard with the girls, put their feet up on my couch, someone I clearly trusted!

Mr Parks Now look/

Sidney Thomas Crane? Archie Thane? Musa Andrew? It's got to be someone close, like really close, right?

Mr Parks Poitier?

Sidney Daniel David? Sammy Davis Jnr? Andrew Inca? Farrar D? Andrew? Andrew Inca? It's Andrew, isn't it?

Mr Parks No.

Sidney Don't lie to me, don't you dare! Let me see that document.

Mr Parks Poitier!

Sidney *tries to snatch it.* **Parks** *wrestles it off from him.*

Sidney You gotta tell me what kind of trouble I'm in, Mr Parks!

Mr Parks In this climate you can't afford to trust anyone but me. Now sit down.

Sidney *remains standing, then relents and takes a seat.*

Mr Parks I wake up Monday morning with a call from NBC producers saying they've just spoken to none other than John G Keenan, ring a bell?

Sidney No! Should it?

Mr Parks He's the Big Daddy'O at Red Channels. AKA the Bible of the Blacklisted. You heard of 'em?

Sidney Yes, no, I don't know, I can't think/

Mr Parks The report of Communist influence in radio and television. They say John has just showed them the list a week before it goes to print, regular arrangement that they have. And in the Negro section they see Sidney Poitier, flashing bright-eyed and bushy-tailed. They're asking me if there's anything I can do to prove you're not a crazy radical. You see, in a perfect world, an artist would stay out of trouble and have a successful career without any hiccups. But the truth is that accidents, naivety and sticky situations are a part of life. When things get too much for a studio to handle, they call Larry Parks to come to their rescue. I sort everything from high-profile abortions to homosexuality coverups. I fix shit and when I fix shit, shit stays fixed. So, I say leave it with me.

Sidney I've been Red-baited/

Mr Parks Looks like it.

Sidney But it's a lie. I shouldn't be on the list I'm obviously being smeared and/

Mr Parks A lie will make it around the world before the truth has time to put on its shoes. Fact is that once accused, you have little chance of exoneration.

Sidney So we just have to accept that this is just an old-fashioned witch hunt then?

Mr Parks We're all witch hunters if the witches are Communists, right? I would like to see them all back in the Soviet Union, wouldn't you?

Sidney *tries to compose himself; he can't quite believe what's happening to him.*

Mr Parks NBC are scared. They think employing you will bring serious accusations and repercussions to their sponsors.

Sidney ... But ...

Mr Parks Look, they don't wanna make a film with a suspected Commy cos that makes them a suspected Commy/

Sidney That does not make sense/

Mr Parks It doesn't but it does, you think the studios are the boss? The sponsors are king; they withdraw their money the studio doesn't have a pot to piss in.

Sidney So what now?

Mr Parks The network won't employ you until you repudiate that behaviour.

Sidney What? Mr Parks, I need this opportunity I/

Mr Parks I know! So, I told them I'll draw up an oath, like a guarantee just stating that you'll pick your friends wisely and you'll stop airing your dirty laundry in public, and here we have it, BOOM!, like magic.

A slightly shaken **Sidney** *takes a look over the document.*

Sidney *I the actor, has not and will not lend my aid, support, advice, counsel or influence on the Communist party.*

Mr Parks I don't need to hear it I wrote it!

Sidney *begins to read it in his head.*

Sidney On?! . . . *'I the actor has not been cautioned for engaging in any behaviour in the past or at any time in the future, which the Company'/*

Mr Parks Poitier?

Sidney How am I supposed to know everything I have engaged in in the past or will engage in the future?

Mr Parks *pulls the oath back.*

Mr Parks You know what, I'm tired of doing the impossible for the unthankful.

Sidney *pulls it back.*

Sidney I sign this, it pleases NBC, and it gets me off the Red Channels, right?

Mr Parks Almost. Mr Keenan says a small public statement will do, will prove your loyalty to the nation in its time of need, and get them off your back for good.

Sidney You never mentioned any statement?

Mr Parks Nothing major, it's all protocol.

Sidney What am I stating?

Mr Parks I've already hooked up a 30-second slot for you on WNYC radio in (*checks the clock*) an hour.

Sidney An hour?

Mr Parks Prime time for the Beatniks.

Sidney Wait, what?

Mr Parks And a page 5 column in *The Times* for the bourgeois and page 6 in *The Crisis* for the regular Coloured folk.

Sidney Slow down.

Mr Parks Keep up.

Sidney What am I stating?

Mr Parks A denouncement of a known Communist.

Sidney Why?

Mr Parks To prove that you're not one.

Sidney . . . Who? Who Parks? Who?

Mr Parks Robeson!

Silence.

Paul Robeson . . .

Silence. This hits **Sidney** *like a ton of bricks.*

Don't look at me like that, Poitier, he's a big fish, they're hungry, give them a big fish to feed on. They'll love you for it.

Sidney I . . . I . . . I.

Mr Parks Relax. I'm a million streets ahead, baby, listen to this: (*Pulls out a new document from his desk drawer and begins to read a statement.*)

'I Sidney Poitier, know of a fanatic who is desperately trying to undermine the Constitution of the United States by depriving artists and others of Life, Liberty, and the Pursuit of Happiness without due process of law. His name is Paul Leroy Robeson. Robeson has been entangled with groups of ex-Fascists and

America-Firsters and anti-Semites, people who hate everybody, including Negros, minority groups, and most likely themselves. Such people are engaged in a conspiracy outside all the legal processes to undermine the very fundamental American concepts upon which our entire system of democracy exists. And neither I nor any member of my Negro community condones such behaviour.'

Is that too long? Needs to be 30 seconds. Feel free to add a little flavour to it. What do you think?

Sidney What the hell is this?

Mr Parks I know, right! The devil works hard but I work harder.

Sidney You've lost your damn mind.

Mr Parks Gratitude, Poitier. I took a long time putting that together.

Sidney Gratitude? Where's your gratitude to a man like Paul Robeson. A man that has built schools with his bare hands or raised awareness for the plight of the Negro in America, to the Welsh miners, or, the struggles in South Africa, or, for being a Black polymath when the terms are assumed to be contradictory. He's the kind of man that pelts stones at giants. Give him some damn gratitude/

Mr Parks You're a day away from having your name displayed in Red Channels, it's play or be played/

Sidney How would *you* sleep at night knowing that you had just destroyed a man's career/

Mr Parks With my drawers down in case he wanted to kiss my ass.

Sidney MR PARKS!

Mr Parks This is not any man, this is an enemy of mainstream America.

Silence.

Mr Parks Imagine, Poitier. They're willing to offer you as much as your eyes can see, all you need to do is repent of any official stand you may have taken with known Commies 'during a stage of child-like-naivety', then repent all those activities under your name in Red Channels and to swear lifelong hatred and opposition to the Communist Party, now surely that can't be too much to ask?

Sidney *sits and thinks about it.*

Sidney There just has to be another way.

Mr Parks They got my nuts in a vice, trust me, this is the best I can do for you, kid.

Silence. A moment where **Mr Parks** *decides to change tack.*

Mr Parks G'head sign the oath and take the statement with you. I got a car on the way to take you to the radio station.

Sidney What? Wait, hold on, I need to think.

Mr Parks The problem is you're thinking too hard! Let me do that for you, doll-face.

Sidney I need to talk to Bobby.

Mr Parks Why talk to Bobby when you're talking to me? He's as dumb as a soup sandwich.

Sidney *tries to gather some headspace.*

Sidney Thank you for your generosity, Mr Parks, but I'm here to make movies and if that's not on the agenda then I'm out.

Mr Parks Yea?

Sidney Yea!

Mr Parks Well, Sorry for wasting your time.

Sidney *makes to leave.*

Mr Parks Expect a letter in the post.

Sidney Please, just leave me alone.

Mr Parks Likelihood is you'll be subpoenaed to testify at the next House of Un-American Activities Committee on suspicion of holding Communist loyalties or being involved in subversive activities.

Sidney What?

Mr Parks You surprised; don't tell me you're surprised?

Sidney What did you say?

Mr Parks Red Channels goes to print tomorrow, goes to press bright and early Monday morning, Hedda Hopper puts it in her column by Wednesday, gets that out to her 35-million-strong audience by Thursday, studio cancels your Deal Memo by Friday, should have your subpoena waiting for you in the Monday morning post. Shit! Is that an eventful week, or is that an eventful week?

Mr Parks *pours two glasses then takes a seat.*

I know more about your tomorrow than you know about your yesterday . . . Sit your little brown butt down, Poitier. Sit those little chicken legs down.

Sidney *slowly goes and takes a seat, then sits there with his head in his hands.*

Mr Parks You OK?

Sidney I think I'm going to be sick.

Mr Parks *pours more Scotch and slides it down the table for* **Sidney**.

Mr Parks Here, sip on this, it'll cancel itself out.

Sidney If I say no?/

Mr Parks Blacklisted! And being blacklisted ain't no joke when you're already Black. You'll be Black-blacklisted. Double black!

Sidney Are you finding this amusing?

Mr Parks You refuse to testify? You'll be canned for contempt.

Sidney Prison?

Mr Parks You dig?

Sidney Prison? You say it like it's routine.

Mr Parks It is. Straight-no-chaser.

Silence.

Sidney How do I know that my name is even on that list, Mr Parks?

Mr Parks You really wanna wait to find out?

Sidney *stumbles over to the window for fresh air.*

Mr Parks Listen here. A clever man solves a problem, a wise man avoids it . . . you can avoid this, Poitier, be wise damn it.

Silence.

Mr Parks *picks up his phone from his desk.*

Mr Parks Maggy, Maggy let my 12 o'clock know I'll meet him in the lobby!!!

Sidney What are you doing?

Mr Parks I don't think there is much else to do but call it a day.

Sidney What?

Mr Parks Thank you, and I wish you all the best, kid, God knows you're gonna need it.

Sidney Is that all?

Mr Parks Look, I'm a businessman, you're a businessman, we're here to talk business, show-business, and it looks like our conversation has ended, just as your future in this business has.

Sidney Mr Parks?

Mr Parks G'head, leave here with hope in one hand and shit in the other and see which gets full faster.

Sidney Let's talk.

Mr Parks No.

Sidney No?

Mr Parks Not until I know you're willing to work with me. I'm no rookie, Poitier, I've been making deals in this industry before your folks were making whoopee! I'm as good as they get and I know my worth. I can't make you sign anything, but by God I wish you would.

Sidney *nods his head.*

Sidney OK.

Mr Parks OK?

Sidney OK.

Mr Parks OK OK?

Sidney I said OK!

Mr Parks *takes the contract back out.* **Sidney** *starts looking through the contract.* **Mr Parks** *slides him a pen.*

Mr Parks *lights up a smoke. He slides one to* **Sidney** *with the light.* **Sidney** *is shaking so much he can't light the smoke.* **Mr Parks** *comes over and helps.*

Sidney Thank you.

Sidney *takes a puff then pulls the contract over to him.*

Sidney *picks up the pen and continues to read, looking for where he must sign.*

KNOCK KNOCK (the door). **Bobby** *walks in.*

Mr Parks What the hell are you doing back here?

Bobby Wow it's hot, hotter than a well digger's ass in here.

Mr Parks Go fry ice, we're busy.

Bobby Why'd it all go silent?

Mr Parks Were you listening to us?

Bobby No . . . Yeah, a little bit . . .

Mr Parks Get out!

Bobby Sid, you all signed up, buddy?

Sidney *takes a deep look at the contract, then at* **Mr Parks**, *then at* **Bobby**. *He's unsure of what's happening and who to trust right now.*

Sidney I think I need some air.

Mr Parks No, wait, come on, Poitier, we're in the middle of a conversation here.

Sidney I need some air!

Sidney *makes to leave,* **Bobby** *attempts to console him.* **Sidney** *steps away from him, then leaves.*

Bobby What's got into him? What did you say?

Mr Parks Wait, Poitier, hey come on, Poitier, wait . . .

Mr Parks *runs after* **Sidney**. **Bobby** *takes a seat and notices the paperwork; he begins leafing through it.*

Mr Parks *returns to the office.*

Mr Parks As an outsider, what's your view on intelligence?

Bobby What's with this denouncement shit?

Mr Parks None of your business, how I do what I do.

Bobby It is if you do it on my movie. It was my thinking that you would get Sidney in, show him the offer, no one resists cos you're irresistible, and kapiche-kapow happy days we all drink champagne and enjoy the sunshine. He doesn't look like he's enjoying the sunshine, Mr Parks, and I don't taste champagne on my lips.

Mr Parks Who. The. Heck do you think you are?

Bobby I don't need my movie involved in your Red Channels, political espionage, sounding bullshit, OK?

Mr Parks Bobby-Brass-Balls has arrived ladies and gentlemen.

Bobby I'm warning you.

Mr Parks You don't warn me you little lily-livered buttercup boy, you're all show and no go. The kind of man that cuts the crusts off his sandwiches, kinda man that takes a piss sitting down.

Bobby I mean it, Parks, don't fuck me, and don't fuck my movie/

Mr Parks The kind of man that lets producers roll you over, tickle your belly and slap you in the face with your own penis, and you think you can come in here talking TO ME like that?

Bobby Sorry, I need my dumbrella it's raining stupid in here.

Mr Parks I'll slap you so cross-eyed you'll eat off other people's plates.

Bobby I wish a bag of shit would hit you in the face.

Mr Parks Looks like it already hit you first!

The men square up to one another. **Bobby** *remembers himself and backs down.*

Bobby Listen to me. A loyalty oath is one thing. But if Sid denounces Robeson's name, then that's it . . . all everybody talking are gonna wanna talk about, is 'Sidney Poitier vs Paul Robeson'. I can see it now, in all the headlines, in all the interviews, yapping about the war on communism and 'Will he be willing to take Robeson's name all the way to the HUAC?' It's a distraction, Mr Parks, and I've come way too far to be distracted. Fuck that! I don't need that type of attention, OK?

Mr Parks 'You don't'?

Bobby *We* don't, my movie. Sid's not reading this ridiculous denouncement shit. He's a good guy and he is loyal; I can vouch for that. Do your dirty work somewhere else, Parks, I'm gonna find Sidney and head out.

Bobby *makes to leave.*

Mr Parks If Poitier doesn't sign. You're in trouble, kid!

Bobby Bullshit!

Mr Parks What you think I'm just gonna act like I haven't seen and heard what I've seen and heard? He's rebellious, with un-American ideologies, and a back catalogue of friends to match. He refuses to denounce a very well-known Commy-ally, and suspiciously turns down the Phoenix project; that would have offered him more money than he's ever seen in his miserable life. You have to admit I've drawn up quite an impressive case.

Silence.

Bobby You said if Sidney doesn't sign, *I'm* in trouble, what's this have to do with me?

Mr Parks On the basis of given evidence, if I were to be an *unbiased witness*, I would be forced to suggest that you seem to be complicit in this conspiracy.

Bobby Your ass must be pretty jealous of all the shit that comes out of your mouth.

Mr Parks (*sings*) *You're buddies, you're tight, your wives watch NBC together on Saturday nights.* You see a throughline here? You've known about his possible Communist affiliations and idolisation of Paul Robeson and made a decision to not come forward and give his name. It would be unlawful of me to say nothing, I mean, it would be un-American.

Bobby Parks??

Mr Parks Knowing how much the studio are trying to keep their image clean, I mean, it seems to be the single most important thing right now, even more important than shitty movies.

Bobby You like the sound of your own voice, don't you?/

Mr Parks You like the sound of your own name?/

Bobby You bet I like it/

Mr Parks Well, you're gonna have to start putting a pseudonym on your scripts if you wanna write another namby-pamby picture.

Bobby . . .?

Mr Parks Dalton Trumbo, Charlie Chaplin, Orson Welles, The Hollywood Ten. Since this movement began, we have seen powerful men fall faster than the loose leaves in the fall. Upside is, this is the closest you'll ever get to be mentioned in the same breath as them.

Bobby You wouldn't give my name, you couldn't.

Mr Parks I would. I literally just said that I would.

Bobby We've always had an understanding.

Mr Parks I wouldn't give you the steam off my shit.

Bobby You've known me for years/

Mr Parks All I know is loyalty to my country.

Bobby Give me a loyalty oath then, I'll sign it.

Mr Parks You're a day late and a dollar short/

Bobby OK, OK, OK, alright . . . Shit! Shit! Shit! . . .

Bobby *takes a moment to think.*

What if he doesn't sign anything? What if we just recast?

Mr Parks What?!! He's your pal.

Bobby He'll understand.

Mr Parks You've written the role for a coloured man?

Bobby Then we just find another, you must know a ton, right?

Mr Parks No!

Bobby No?

Mr Parks No.

Bobby No, you don't or no we don't?

Mr Parks You know what, it would be easier to replace you instead.

Bobby What are you/

Mr Parks Just replace you with another up-and-coming square schmuck. A good guy, a yes sir, three bags full sir, kinda man, no complications. I know a few, I'll make some recommendations.

Bobby Are you suffering from insanity?

Mr Parks No I'm enjoying every second of it.

Bobby This is my baby!

Mr Parks Not your name on the birth certificate. This script is NBC property. You're an employee, also NBC property. It's all in the contracts. Why does nobody ever read the damn contracts?

Bobby I need this movie/

Mr Parks What you NEED is to start thinking smart!

Bobby OK, OK, please. Help me!

Mr Parks First things first, no recast.

Bobby Why?

Mr Parks Poitier's the only one that's gonna do this movie. We'll make sure of that OK?/

Bobby Why does it have to be Sidney?

Mr Parks Dumb down, Bobby. Every man likes a little-ass nobody likes a smart-ass.

Bobby You need him.

Mr Parks *You* need him!

Bobby But why? Why??!!

Bobby *takes a second to try and look* **Mr Parks** *in the eyes for an answer.* **Mr Parks** *retreats.*

Bobby You don't give a damn about whether Sid does this movie or not.

Mr Parks Knock it off, kid.

Bobby But somebody does. Who? What's going on, Parks? Who keeps calling? I'm not as stupid as *you* look.

Mr Parks Less you know the better.

Bobby The Mob?

Mr Parks What the hell do the Mob want with Preacher-suit-Poitier?

Bobby So Senator McCarthy?

Mr Parks McCarthy's small fish in comparison.

Silence. **Mr Parks** *looks intensely at the clock; he's running out of time.* **Bobby** *sits on the table with his arms crossed, he's not budging without an answer.* **Mr Parks** *goes over to the door to make sure no one can hear what he is about to say.*

Mr Parks Look, you piece of piss. There's a lot of concern about the growing power of this new 'civil rights movement'. The FBI is/

Bobby The FBI?/

Mr Parks Ramping up its surveillance of domestic dissidents/

Bobby The FBI, Parks? Have you lost your tits?

Mr Parks No, I have not lost my tits. Paul Robeson continues to travel across the world, attempting to embarrass our nation for being 'guilty of genocide' and then having the audacity to declare that socialism would be the world's best hope for humanity.

Bobby So what!

Mr Parks So what?? There is a real danger that we'll become a goddamn totalitarian dictatorship, and I would rather put my life on the line as a free man than live as a slave, Bobby.

Bobby Robeson is already blacklisted. What more do they need/

Mr Parks To justify it. Prove that he *is* a menace to society and not some sort of Negro Messiah being crucified by the White Man. They need to 'discredit his voice' and nullify his power completely.

Bobby Is this about silencing Paul Robeson or creating a vengeful atmosphere that deters anyone from speaking out?

Mr Parks It's about a battle for the future of American democracy. For men. Men like us.

Bobby So again, I ask, what the hell has this got to do with my movie?

Mr Parks NBC are not the only ones excited by the possibility of a Negro star. The FBI need one too – one that the Blacks respect and that the Whites are growing to belove. One that is in the spotlight, that loves Robeson and looks up to him, idolises him, and even publicly knows the guy. Poitier is their guy. This is his break.

Bobby We just gonna sit and watch the FBI infiltrate our industry?

Mr Parks Who would you prefer, Hoover or Stalin?

Bobby Is this shit even legal?

Mr Parks What kind of question/

Bobby IS THIS LEGAL?

Mr Parks Who cares about law?

Bobby You're a lawyer!

Mr Parks Don't ask if it's legal, ask if it's right, because/

Bobby Is it right?

Mr Parks Don't ask me that crap. All you need to know is that NBC needs to silence Poitier and the FBI need him to speak. This Loyalty Oath and the Denouncement is my way of killing one bird with two stones.

Bobby What are you getting out of this?

Mr Parks I'm a good Samaritan.

Bobby And a bad liar.

Mr Parks I'm trying to help my country in its time of need.

Bobby Bullshit!! How much are the FBI paying you?

Mr Parks Bobby-baby-really? What do you take me for?

Bobby How much?

Mr Parks Enough for a six-month vacation twice a year.

Bobby Parks, you'll regret this in the morning.

Mr Parks Then I'll sleep till noon.

Bobby You're a two-bit/

Mr Parks Man! I'm a man, a real one, taking care of me and mine. I'm thinking fast about the future, like you should be. Look around you, at any given moment some dumb dolphin might roll through this office with our names in his pocket, wanting to squeal about something we said, or did all the way back when we were knee-high to a grasshopper. The world is changing and I wanna go out the same way I came in. I refuse to be anybody's slave, Bobby . . .

Silence whilst **Bobby** *takes in* **Mr Parks'** *level of paranoia.*

Mr Parks Look here. You make this . . . *wonderful* movie, Poitier becomes the first Black actor to lead a prime-time drama and becomes a star. We let them take down Paul Robeson once and for all, and I enhance my reputation whilst making some serious bang for my buck. And all while upholding American values, right, Bobby son?

The phone rings. **Mr Parks** *answers:* Hello? OK.

Mr Parks *slams the phone back down.*

Mr Parks He's on his way back up.

Bobby Shit. Shit!

Mr Parks Now look at me, I've gone in and played bad cop, now the stage is set for you.

Bobby I, but I/

Mr Parks Calm down and balls-up! Listen to me and you'll have him begging to sign it.

Bobby Look/

Mr Parks Be nice, Bobby, be really nice, let him vent about his feelings, and emotions, let him get really plummy. Let him know that you share the same shit just different toilet, you dig?

Mr Parks *begins to smarten* **Bobby** *up.*

Mr Parks And Bobby.

Bobby Yes Mr Parks?

Mr Parks You got ten mins to save your career . . .

Bobby God. Damn . . .

Silence.

Mr Parks Come on in, Poitier.

Sidney *opens the door, looking very distraught and sweaty.*

Bobby *stares at the clock. Everyone in the room stands, taking shape as though it were a Texas showdown.*

Sidney I need to talk to Bobby.

Mr Parks Well you're in luck cos he wants to speak to you also. You love birds play nice!

Bobby Hey Sid . . . feeling any better now?

Mr Parks *looks at the clock and then leaves.*

Long silence.

Sidney You know what they're asking me to do?

Bobby No, I mean, yes, well kind of. You gonna do it?

Sidney . . .

Bobby If you want my two cents, Sid, you know, I mean it's not like you'll be the first, or the last, to give his name.

Sidney That doesn't make it right, Bobby.

Bobby Jackie Robinson's just been recommended to the Veterans of Foreign Wars for good citizenship. Giving Robeson's name seems to have worked out OK for him, right? Going into a big movie, that's the type of good PR you could do with, buddy

Sidney You seen Jackie walking around the streets of Harlem lately?

Bobby You think the Blacks will call you a sell-out?

Sidney Paul is nothing short of an icon and/

Bobby Ahhh. What! You'd be capitalizing on an opportunity that doesn't make you a sell-out, does it? Nope! It's/

Sidney When you completely go against everything you stood for, becoming addicted to making money hand over fist/

Bobby There's a difference in being addicted to money and knowing that you can't live without it, because you can't, Sidney. The best thing you can do for the poor Blacks is to not be one of them.

Silence. **Sidney** *is dead still, deep in thought.* **Bobby** *doesn't quite know if he is getting through so tries a different approach.*

Bobby I think Isla's leaving me, Sid.

Sidney What?

Bobby ...

Sidney What happened?

Bobby She's 'addicted to money' and I'm running out of it.

They both share a laugh.

Sidney You're ridiculous.

Bobby Seriously, though, it's high time for me to show that I can truly be a provider. Only women and children get loved unconditionally. We men? We are loved only under the condition that we provide. That's the measure of a man. My father taught me that.

Sidney 'A man without provision is a man without purpose' – mine would say something similar. But/

Bobby Exactly! You and I, Sid, we're not that different. Your parents came from the tomato fields of the Bahamas. Mine were migrant workers who came to this country after the Great War. They were stoic, principled, made sacrifices, made some enemies too, but they always, always, put family first. And that's what brings true happiness. That's what you're signing up for, Sid. If not for you, then for your family.

Silence.

Sidney Then what am I missing, Bobby? I feel terrible. Am I wrong to feel this way?

Bobby It's not about wrong or right.

Sidney But am I wrong?

Bobby It's about staying afloat and not burning bridges.

Sidney Bobby/

Bobby You can be right and still burn bridges, Sidney. I know your head and heart are in a good place, but you have to look out for the girls, the baby on the way. You have a family now/

Sidney I know what I have/

Bobby Then protect it. And protect them! We both know the cost of coming from nothing and how it would be absolutely unimaginable to take our loved ones back there.

Sidney But I cannot/

Bobby Watch everything that we've achieved, watch everyone that is rooting for us, counting on us just waste away for the sake of some damn integrity. . .

Sidney . . . I just/

Bobby Need to allow them to lift you up or watch them tear you down, I don't think we can have it both ways, Sidney. You walked away from the Phoenix project, good for you, well done, but you don't walk away from a network and live to tell the tale. If you tell your boss to go fuck-shit, you better have a back-up plan . . . What's the point of principles if you don't have a platform? Why make provocative work if no one gets to see it? The industry has closed their doors to me and won't even open it for you. This is our chance, Sid.

Sidney What does it profit a man to gain the whole world and lose his soul?

Bobby The world, Sidney! The whole mother-fucking world!

Sidney *takes a moment, taken back,* **Bobby** *doubles down.*

Bobby 'What am I going to give not what am I going to get.' This industry will not respond to you unless you are ready to give something. To make a sacrifice.

Sidney *jumps up, he feels uncomfortable, like something isn't right about the way* **Bobby** *is speaking.*

Sidney (*confused*) . . . You're quoting Parks now?

Bobby (*laughs*) Maybe the man has a point or two, right Sid?

Sidney Am I your sacrifice?

Bobby What??

Sidney If I say no, will you be denouncing my name?

Bobby Excuse me?

Sidney Answer the question.

Bobby If you know me, I shouldn't have to/

Sidney How well does anyone know anyone anymore?

Bobby Sidney, you know I would never/

Sidney What were you and Parks just talking about?

Bobby I . . . I was defending you.

Sidney And before I came in this morning?

Bobby I was telling him how great you are.

Sidney What did Parks offer you for your sins? A Ford convertible? A room full of hookers? Thirty pieces of silver?

Bobby Now you're out of line here!

Sidney Tell me I'm lying?

Bobby You're my friend.

Sidney And this is an opportunity of a lifetime.

Bobby I'm a lot of shitty little things but a rat ain't one of 'em!

Sidney We once said we were going to change the world together, and now you've let it change you. What happened Bobby, you got tired?

Bobby Tired? Changed me? Seriously? The only reason I'm still here is to prove that you're not who they think you might be. To make sure you don't prove them right, to make sure you don't say or do some stupid shit that would get your ass fired, before you're even hired. It's like you've been in the struggle so long you don't know who you are without it, you can't see friend from foe. You can't see how close you are to some good, to history in the making, Sidney! We spoke about the problems Negros face in this industry, the types of roles that would be progressive, you and I, Sid, and *I* came up with solutions.

Sidney And don't we all know about it!

Bobby How dare you!

Sidney Hail Bobby my Lord and Saviour!

Silence. **Bobby** *is seething.*

Bobby All you've had to do is be cool, be calm, play along, nod and smile, drink the man's drink when he offers you, learn to self-censor from controversial outbursts that you know have now become associated with communism, sign a god damn contract, do a bit of radio and, happy days, we get to make a whole fucking movie something bigger than the conversation on race, something bigger than ourselves! But you can't do it, you find a way, you find a way of complicating this, complicating everything, you always find a way, Sid, and I don't understand why you can't just do what you're told!!!

Sidney ... Because quite obviously the lack of unity in America is caused by my unwillingness to kiss the ass of those that make my life a living hell ...

Bobby Cut it out, Sidney. I've done so fucking much work so you wouldn't come across as some stereotypical angry/

Sidney I am angry, Bobby! The type of anger that manifests when you have been so angry that you're literally burning up inside, you're burning up with rage, you're about to blow a fuse, but don't. You can't. You come to learn that *you* must find positive outlets for anger or it will destroy you physically, destroy everyone you come into contact with; because it reaches such intensity that to express it fully would require homicidal rage, self-destructive, destroy the whole fucking world-type rage, and its flame burns because the world is so unjust. You ever been that angry, Bobby? So angry that you have to find a way to channel that anger to the positive, because you never have the luxury of just being a man! Every move you make is tantamount to the representation of 18 million people. So, you're forced to be careful and tread so lightly that you could never ever, not even for a second amount to that stereotype that they oh-so want you to be. So be well groomed, well-spoken, don't move too fast, smile till your face hurt, near choke yourself to death in this suit, damn it!!! I'm tired of playing the good little Negro, that's not a character I signed up for! I'm tired of living my life in such a way to make white people 'comfortable'.

Silence.

I do not need any more of your 'solutions', Bobby. All I ever wanted was your genuine support and solidarity. I wanted you to know how being an American for a Black man can be both a source of pride and pain. To understand the harm caused by discrimination and join me in speaking out against injustice and inequity, but not speak for me . . . I know what I have to do for myself and for my family, Bobby, but I guess I just wanted you to understand why being forced to denounce possibly the greatest man I've ever met, will be one of the most heartbreaking things I will ever have to do, and not dismiss my fears, but cry with me when racism and hatred win . . . That's all . . . so . . .

Sidney *begins to tear up.* **Bobby** *takes a moment to let what* **Sidney** *has said sink in, then he moves to console him, but* **Sidney** *moves away, not ready for that yet.*

Silence.

Mr Parks *enters the room to a sombre affair.*

Mr Parks It's been a funny old morning . . . Champagne and cigars, how about it?

Sidney How about it.

Sidney *looks away.* **Bobby** *reluctantly nods his head 'Yes'.* **Mr Parks** *smiles, then slides the contracts back over.*

Mr Parks Yes!

Mr Parks *goes to his cabinet to retrieve a box of cigars.* **Sidney** *takes the contract and a pen.*

Bobby Sid, you sure about this?

Sidney We'll let history be the final judge.

Mr Parks *pours the drinks, distributes the cigars.*

Mr Parks *hands the pen over to* **Sidney**. **Sidney** *takes a seat and prepares to sign the Loyalty Oath.*

Mr Parks You ready?

Sidney . . . Yes sir.

Sidney *begins flicking through the document. Finally, he signs.*

Mr Parks We need to toast this glorious occasion with style! This is good; this is three nice men from completely different walks of life coming together for the good of the country. Fighting for what really matters . . .

Sidney *takes a moment to think about* **Mr Parks**' *comment whilst humming.*

Sidney You ever heard Paul Robeson sing?

Mr Parks Yea beautiful, incredible/

Sidney May 18, 1952, the Peace Arch Concert, that was my first time. US government refused him permission to cross the border/

Mr Parks They seized his passport, I know, and good thing/

Sidney So he sang at the border/

Mr Parks I know the story/

Sidney The crowd at the Peace Arch received upward of 45,000. The people showed up, Mr Parks. About three-fourths of the crowd gathered on Canadian soil and one-fourth on the United States side of the border. We sang 'O Canada' and 'The Star-Spangled Banner'. I knew he was a great actor, but I had never heard the man sing.

Mr Parks Turn off the juice, Poitier/

Sidney He sang in English, songs of peace in Russian and Chinese, songs of liberty in a tongue of the African villages. He had a most wonderful voice, rich and powerful. Chills went down my spine when he spoke, and when he sang, it felt he was singing to you directly.

Mr Parks Now look at me, there's still a job to be done.

Sidney Think about it – The Red Scare, the Korean War, the Cold War raging. And here is a guy with a strong antiwar stand who has been branded as one of the most dangerous men in the world, singing, just singing about peace!

Mr Parks There's a car waiting downstairs to take you to the radio station.

Sidney I was in complete awe, I still am. He puts his life out there where people can reach it and uses his artistry and stature to do good in the world. A courageous giant of a man. That's been my goal as a human being. I can't meet his stature, but I can at least try, right?

Mr Parks Poitier, everyone's entitled to act stupid once in a while, but you're really abusing the privilege. Now, if you don't wanna get in that car, I know a good little greasy spoon that could do with a great actor come rebel come God damn dishwasher. You'll have plenty of time to talk about your heroes there. Now shut your damn mouth and listen to me.

Sidney No, you shut your damn mouth and listen to me.

Silence, everyone is awestruck. **Mr Parks** *turns to* **Bobby**.

Mr Parks You going to let him talk that way?

Bobby I don't know.

Sidney Mr Parks, the problem with you is that you're a fearful, angry, grasping man; you close your eyes, and you hate, hate, hate, hate, hate. And like everybody in a world of hate you're afraid I'm gonna take something away from you, but I got news for you: you ain't got nothing I want. You dig?

I was born two months early, and everyone had given up on me, but my mother insisted on my life. She passed a fortune-teller's stall, and she sat with this lady. The woman said, 'Don't worry about your son. He will not be a sickly child. He will walk with kings. He will step on pillars of gold. And he will carry your name to many places.' Believe that with or without this contract I'm still going to be somebody not just an anybody but my mother's son! Now look at me, look at me, there's a job to be done, and I don't need a single second longer to think about it. There is a movement. Something incredibly remarkable is about to happen, something that this country maybe even this world has never ever seen, and I don't want to miss that I don't want to live a life regretting that I missed that moment. Forgive me, Bobby, and fuck you, Mr Parks, but I do not wish to be on the wrong side of history.

Sidney *rips the contract in two.* **Mr Parks** *mouth drops.*

Mr Parks (*to* **Bobby**) We can't make a silk purse out of a sow's ear. You can't make a gentleman out of a suntanned man! That's all he is, Bobby; I think too many times you forget that. We've failed him, by giving him too much respect. I say g'head, re-cast him, show him who's boss.

Sidney Still catching that train, Bobby?

Sidney *leaves the office. Silence.* **Bobby** *puts on his jacket then proceeds to leave the room. A voiceover of Sidney Poitier's speech is heard, during which the telephone rings.* **Mr Parks** *answers and slams down the receiver, then leaves the office.*

Sidney (*V/O*) I arrived in Hollywood at the age of twenty-two in a time different than today's, a time in which the odds against my standing here tonight, fifty-three years later would not have fallen in my favour. Back then, no route had been established for where I was hoping to go, no pathway left in evidence for me to trace, no custom for me to follow. Yet, here I am this evening at the end of a journey that in 1949 would have been considered almost impossible and in fact might never have been set in motion were there not an untold number of courageous, unselfish choices made by a handful of visionary American filmmakers, directors, writers and producers; each with a strong sense of citizenship responsibility to the times in which they lived; They knew the odds that stood against them and their efforts were overwhelming and likely could have proven too high to overcome. And I've benefited from their effort. The industry benefited from their effort. America benefited from their effort. The world has also benefited from their effort.

During this speech **Sidney** *returns to the stage and smiles at the audience.*

Fade to blackout.

The End.

Discover. Read. Listen. Watch.

A NEW WAY TO ENGAGE WITH PLAYS

This award-winning digital library features over 3,000 playtexts, 400 audio plays, 300 hours of video and 360 scholarly books.

Playtexts published by Methuen Drama, The Arden Shakespeare, Faber & Faber, Playwrights Canada Press, Aurora Metro Books and Nick Hern Books.

Audio Plays from L.A. Theatre Works featuring classic and modern works from the oeuvres of leading American playwrights.

Video collections including films of live performances from the RSC, The Globe and The National Theatre, as well as acting masterclasses and BBC feature films and documentaries.

FIND OUT MORE:
www.dramaonlinelibrary.com • @dramaonlinelib

Methuen Drama Modern Plays

include

Bola Agbaje
Edward Albee
Ayad Akhtar
Jean Anouilh
John Arden
Peter Barnes
Sebastian Barry
Clare Barron
Alistair Beaton
Brendan Behan
Edward Bond
William Boyd
Bertolt Brecht
Howard Brenton
Amelia Bullmore
Anthony Burgess
Leo Butler
Jim Cartwright
Lolita Chakrabarti
Caryl Churchill
Lucinda Coxon
Tim Crouch
Shelagh Delaney
Ishy Din
Claire Dowie
David Edgar
David Eldridge
Dario Fo
Michael Frayn
John Godber
James Graham
David Greig
John Guare
Lauren Gunderson
Peter Handke
David Harrower
Jonathan Harvey
Robert Holman
David Ireland
Sarah Kane
Barrie Keeffe
Jasmine Lee-Jones
Anders Lustgarten
Duncan Macmillan
David Mamet
Patrick Marber
Martin McDonagh
Arthur Miller
Alistair McDowall
Tom Murphy
Phyllis Nagy
Anthony Neilson
Peter Nichols
Ben Okri
Joe Orton
Vinay Patel
Joe Penhall
Luigi Pirandello
Stephen Poliakoff
Lucy Prebble
Peter Quilter
Mark Ravenhill
Philip Ridley
Willy Russell
Jackie Sibblies Drury
Sam Shepard
Martin Sherman
Chris Shinn
Wole Soyinka
Simon Stephens
Kae Tempest
Anne Washburn
Laura Wade
Theatre Workshop
Timberlake Wertenbaker
Roy Williams
Snoo Wilson
Frances Ya-Chu Cowhig
Benjamin Zephaniah

For a complete listing of
Methuen Drama titles, visit:
www.bloomsbury.com/drama

Follow us on Twitter and keep up to date
with our news and publications
@MethuenDrama